W9-AWK-691

NO LONGER THE PROPERTY OF
BALDWIN PUBLIC LIBRARY

Eat Well

Angela Royston

BALDWIN PUBLIC LIBRARY

Heinemann Library
Des Plaines, Illinois

© 2000 Reed Educational & Professional Publishing
Published by Heinemann Library,
an imprint of Reed Educational & Professional Publishing,
1350 East Touhy Avenue, Suite 240 West
Des Plaines, IL 60018

Customer Service 1-888-454-2279

All rights reserved. No part of this publication may be reproduced or transmitted in any form or by any means, electronic or mechanical, including photocopying, recording, taping, or any information storage and retrieval system, without permission in writing from the publisher.

Text designed by Celia Floyd
Illustrations by Barry Atkinson
Printed and bound in Hong Kong,China

04 03 02 01 00
10 9 8 7 6 5 4 3 2 1

Library of Congress Cataloging-in-Publication Data
Royston, Angela.
    Eat Well / Angela Royston.
        p. cm. – (Safe and sound)
    Includes bibliographical references and index.
    Summary: Presents the food pyramid and discusses the roles of various types of nutrients, such as carbohydrates, sugars, and proteins, in maintaining good health.
    ISBN 1-57572-982-2
    1. Nutrition Juvenile literature. [1. Nutrition.] I. Title.
    II. Series: Royston, Angela. Safe and Sound.
    QP141.R73 1999
    613.2—dc21   99-14553
                                                  CIP

Acknowledgments
The Publishers would like to thank the following for permission to reproduce photographs: Bubbles/F. Rombout, p. 16; L. Thurston, p. 29; Trevor Clifford, pp. 8–11, 13–15, 17–19, 21–28; Richard Greenhill, p. 12; PowerStock, p. 5; Science Photo Library/A. Bartel, p. 4; Tony Stone Images/ B. Stablyk, p. 20.

Cover photo: Trevor Clifford.

Every effort has been made to contact copyright holders of any material reproduced in this book. Any omissions will be rectified in subsequent printings if notice is given to the Publisher.

The Publishers would like to thank Julie Johnson, PSHE consultant and trainer, for her comments in the preparation of this book.

Some words in this book are in bold, **like this**. You can find out what they mean by looking in the glossary.

449 – 3390

Contents

Enjoy Your Meal!

Food helps you stay healthy and well. It tastes good. It keeps you from feeling hungry. Different foods help your body in different ways.

This book tells you about the different kinds of food your body needs. Some foods give you **energy**. Other foods help you grow strong.

Food Pyramid

The food **pyramid** shows how much of each different kind of food you should eat every day. It shows the basic food groups: **grains,** vegetables, fruit, milk, meat, and **fats** and sweets.

The foods in each part of the pyramid help your body in different ways. All of the food groups are important for a healthy body, but your body needs more of some foods than others.

You should eat more of the foods at the bottom and the middle of the pyramid. You should eat less of the foods at the top.

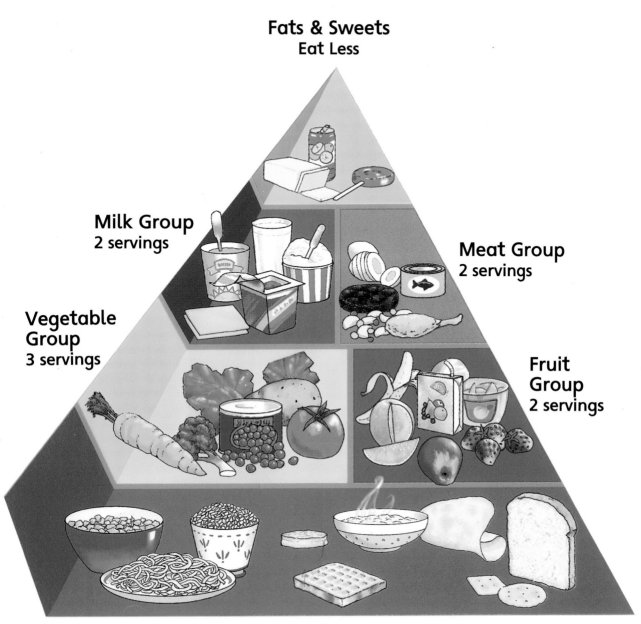

Fats & Sweets
Eat Less

Milk Group
2 servings

Meat Group
2 servings

Vegetable
Group
3 servings

Fruit
Group
2 servings

Grain Group 6 servings

Based on the Food Guide Pyramid for Young Children, U.S. Department of Agriculture,
Center for Nutrition Policy and Promotions, March 1999.

7

A Healthy Mixture

What is your favorite food? Pizza gives you food from each part of the food **pyramid.**

To keep healthy, you should eat a mixture of food from each part of the pyramid. This snack gives you one serving from the fruit group and one serving from the milk group.

Energy Food

All of these foods contain **carbohydrates**. Your body needs this kind of food to make **energy**.

Everything you do uses up energy—moving, chewing, even the beating of your **heart**. Eating a thick slice of toast gives you energy.

Fruit and Vegetables

Make sure you eat five servings a day of fruit and vegetables. They contain **vitamins, minerals,** and **fiber,** which all help keep you healthy.

Raw carrot is sweet and has lots of fiber. It also has vitamins A and C. They keep your skin and eyes healthy, and they help your body fight **disease**.

13

Fiber

Food goes into your stomach. The parts of the food your body needs pass into your **blood**. The rest passes out of your body when you go to the toilet.

These foods all contain **fiber**. Eating food with fiber in it helps your body get rid of waste.

Proteins

Your body is growing all the time. **Proteins** are special kinds of food. They help build new **bone**, skin, **muscle,** and other parts of your body.

Meat, fish, cheese, and beans all contain proteins. Eating these foods will help your body grow bigger.

Calcium

Calcium is a **mineral** that helps build strong **bones** and teeth. Milk contains calcium. Yogurt and cheese are made from milk, so they contain calcium, too.

Broccoli and other green vegetables also contain this important mineral. Some foods and drinks have calcium added to them.

Fatty Food

Hot dogs, hamburgers, ice cream, and many other foods contain **fats**. Your body needs some fat to stay warm, but don't have too much.

Fats give you even more **energy** than **carbohydrates**. Fatty foods taste good, but too much fat can make you unhealthy.

Sugar

Many people like to eat candy, cakes, and cookies. Sweet food and drinks may taste good, but too much sugar can make you unhealthy.

Sugar left in your mouth after eating can hurt your teeth. Remember to brush your teeth after eating or drinking sugary things.

Allergies

Some people cannot eat certain foods because they are **allergic** to them. Milk and cheese make this girl's skin red and itchy.

Peanuts make this girl sick. She always checks the **ingredients** of the things she eats. She has to make sure there are no peanuts in them.

Three Meals a Day?

Most people eat three meals a day. A good breakfast gives you **energy** to start your day. This breakfast mixes food from two food groups.

Some people need to eat several small meals in a day. No matter how many meals you eat, remember to eat a mixture from the food **pyramid.**

Healthy Snacks

When you are hungry between meals, you may want a sugary snack. Think again! Choose a snack that tastes good and is healthy, too.

Popcorn is a healthy snack. It is a **grain,** so it has lots of **carbohydrates.** It is fun to make, too.

Glossary

allergic   to be sick or get a rash after eating some foods or breathing dust or pollen

blood   red liquid that carries food and oxygen around the body

bone   hard part of the body. Bones are connected to give your body its shape.

calcium   substance found in some foods and also in teeth and bones

carbohydrates   parts of food that the body uses to get energy

disease   sickness

energy   to be able and strong enough to do things

fats   parts of some foods that the body uses to get energy and to keep warm

fiber   rough parts of food that pass through the body and help get rid of waste

grain   cereal plant such as wheat or corn

heart   body part that pumps the blood around the body

ingredient   one of many different foods that are in something to eat

mineral   substance the body needs to stay healthy

muscle   part of the body that moves the bones

protein   type of food that the body needs to grow and that can be found in foods such as beans and cheese

pyramid   shape with a flat bottom and triangle sides that come to a point at the top

vitamin   chemical the body needs to change food into energy. There are thirteen vitamins.

Index

More Books to Read

Bryant-Mole, Karen. *Food*. Des Plaines, Ill.: Heinemann Library, 1997.

Patten, Barbara J. *The Basic Five Food Groups*. Vero Beach, Fla.: Rourke Corporation, 1996.

Powell, Jillian. *Food & Your Health*. Austin, Tex.: Raintree Steck-Vaughn, 1998.

BALDWIN PUBLIC LIBRARY

3 1115 00449 3390

NO LONGER THE PROPERTY OF
BALDWIN PUBLIC LIBRARY

J
613.2
R

Royston, Angela.

Eat well.

19.92

DATE			

BALDWIN PUBLIC LIBRARY
2385 GRAND AVE
BALDWIN, NY 11510—3289
(516) 223—6228

BAKER & TAYLOR